Star POWER

FOUR WAYS TO TRANSFORM YOUR VOLUNTEER MINISTRY

HAMP LEE III

(com)mission™

PUBLISHING

STAR Power/Hamp Lee III -- 3rd edition.
ISBN 978-1-940042-03-9

table of CONTENTS

introduction

Since April 1996, I've been a member of numerous churches around the world. I served as a lay member, lay minister, youth pastor, church elder, and pastor. And in almost every church, volunteers were mostly overworked, overlooked, and unappreciated. I've witnessed many people confess Jesus as their Lord and Savior, be baptized, attend a three to six-week New Believer's course (if one was available), and be directly assigned to volunteer in a ministry with little or no training. With only a basic understanding of the Bible and spiritual matters, they're helping to manage ministries.

Though volunteers may be frustrated, tired, and even overwhelmed at times, I truly believe they want to be effective and successful in their service. They want to support the work of God in the church and make a difference in members' lives...and many are.

I also don't believe pastors and church leaders intentionally disregard or neglect their volunteers' needs. I believe they want to be faithful in their calling and to those they lead. However, some church leaders have been so consumed with their ministry operations, schedule, and staffing, that volunteers haven't received more attention and care. Then again there are others that haven't placed much thought on their volunteers' needs because they're only replicating systems and processes they too have experienced over the years.

This is where my discussion for *STAR Power* begins. *STAR Power* highlights four simple ways you can effectively minister to your volunteers. Lord willing, through the topics of Support, Training, Appreciation, and Restoration (STAR), you'll be empowered with foundational tools and principles to care for your volunteer staff.

Ministering to your volunteers is just as important as ministering to your members and visitors. Your volunteers are beautiful souls with personal and spiritual needs, wants, and desires as well. All I ask is that you'll read *STAR Power* with an open mind, a tender heart, and a listening ear. May the few words in this book speak volumes into your life and ministry. Your volunteers need your help and support, and I pray that through *STAR Power*, you'll discover ways to care for those who serve along side you in the Lord's harvest.

support

WHY IS IT IMPORTANT TO SUPPORT VOLUNTEERS?

Depending on the ministry your volunteers serve in, they're often left to manage their area of responsibility with little help or support. They must fend for themselves in a ministry where they may feel undertrained and overwhelmed. This is why it's vitally important to support your volunteers.

Supporting your volunteers is one of the key foundations in building sound ministries in the service of God. This foundation requires you to genuinely care for them, not only in your words, but your actions as well. And for this to happen, you can pray and intercede for them; love them as yourself; understand the issues surrounding their personal and spiritual life; and serve them wholeheartedly.

PRAYER

The importance of prayer cannot be understated. As a church leader, interceding for those within your care should be a top priority. You should make time throughout the day to pray for volunteers' health, personal and spiritual growth, their success in the ministry, and any other issues the Lord places upon your heart (cf. Luke 18:1-7; 1 Thessalonians 5:17). You should also discipline yourself to quietly sit in the Lord's presence to hear what He may share concerning your volunteers' issues and specific needs.

LOVE

When a lawyer sought to tempt Jesus, he asked what was the greatest commandment in the law. Jesus answered:

Thou shalt love the Lord thy God with all thy heart, and with all thy soul, and with all thy mind. This is the first and great commandment. And the second is like unto it, Thou shalt love thy neighbour as thyself. On these two commandments hang all the law and the prophets.

MATTHEW 22:36-40

The Greek translation of the word neighbor is a friend, any other person; according to Christ, any other man irrespective of nation or religion with whom we live or whom we chance to meet.[1] Understanding this, you are to love everyone you meet in the same manner you want to be loved...in *every* situation.

Take a few moments to prayerfully consider the next five questions. Use a journal to record your thoughts and guidance from the Lord.

1. Were you ever discouraged in ministry? If so, please describe your most vivid memory.

2. Do you know how it feels to go weeks or months without attending a church service? If so, please describe your thoughts and feelings in those moments.

3. Have you ever served when you were tired because there was no one else willing to volunteer? If so, please explain.

4. Did you ever experience a lack of support from your church leaders? If so, how did you feel? How did you want them to support you?

5. In what ways can you reciprocate the love you wanted in ministry toward your volunteers?

UNDERSTANDING

Rejoice with them that do rejoice, and weep with them that weep.

ROMANS 12:15

Along with love, many people want to be understood, and your volunteers are no different. If your volunteers come to you with their issues, they may not be searching for solutions (at that moment). They may only want you to understand the issues surrounding their personal and spiritual life. They may simply need someone to talk to...and this is when the opportunity for true ministry begins.

It's important that you know Sally has been depressed because of a pending divorce; Jim has an ailing mother in another state with mounting medical bills; John has lost his job and is scared he'll lose his house; Mary is being abused by her husband; and Terry has car problems and doesn't have enough money to pay for the repairs.

Your volunteers bring similar issues like these to church every week. Their lives aren't divided into neat compartments separate from their church life. Each person is made up of every event and situation they've experienced in their past. It's what makes them who they are and how they interact and respond to other people and situations. And this is where your help and understanding is key.

It'll take a continued investment of your time, patience, and a nonjudgmental attitude to effectively minister to your volunteers. It's important to remain visible, available, and approachable, while creating an environment where comments and ideas can be freely shared.

Every person and situation will be different. How you address one volunteer will be entirely different from the next. Sometimes, you'll address the same volunteer differently based on the circumstances in their life. However, it's important to remain sensitive to the Holy Spirit's direction and guidance. You must be as flexible as a rubber band when ministering to others. Remember: time, patience, and a nonjudgmental attitude.

When you're able to understand your volunteers' issues, they'll slowly begin to open up to you. They'll provide snapshots of who they are and what they're going through. And when appropriate, you'll have the opportunity to provide the necessary clarity to refocus their lives (and situation) back to the Lord, and walk with them as they weather through their storms.

However, not everyone will open up to you. You'll still need to remain available and treat them with love and respect. When I pastored, there were many people unwilling to open up to me. The Lord would tell me what issues they had in their lives, but they didn't feel comfortable speaking to me. Maybe their situation was too embarrassing, pride and sin hindered their path, or they didn't trust people with sensitive details of their lives. Regardless of the reason, I had to continually make myself available and treat them with love and respect. I wouldn't smother them or try to force them to talk to me. I had to respect their 'space,' but I didn't need to be in their 'space' to pray for them. If it was the Lord's will for them to speak with me, it would happen...and I would openly accept them.

SERVICE

But Jesus called them unto him, and said, Ye know that the princes of the Gentiles exercise dominion over them, and they that are great exercise authority upon them. But it shall not be so among you: but whosoever will be great among you, let him be your minister; And whosoever will be chief among you, let him be your servant: Even as the Son of man came not to be ministered unto, but to minister, and to give his life a ransom for many.

MATTHEW 20:25-28

Jesus told His disciples that they were not to exercise dominion over the people as the princes of the Gentiles had done. Sadly however, we find this very thing occurring in many churches today. Some church leaders want to be treated as royalty rather than presenting themselves as humble servants before their congregation. If you want to be the greatest or the chief among your brethren, you should be their minister and servant, regardless of what 'level' of ministry you're leading over.

The Greek word for minister is translated as one who executes the commands of another (esp. of a master, a servant, attendant, minister); the servant of a king; a waiter; a deacon.[2] If you're a minister to your volunteers, you would be attentive to their specific needs (verbal and nonverbal) and be ready to use every resource at your disposal to accomplish each one.

As Jesus didn't come to be ministered to, but to minister, you should emulate His example with those He placed in your care. Jesus has entrusted you with the responsibility of caring for the precious souls He died for. Therefore, pray for them, love them as yourself, understand them, and be their greatest minister and servant.

training

Many churches allow untrained volunteers to run their ministries each week. Sometimes, this has to do with the church leader's lack of experience, understanding on how to execute an effective training program, ineffective training materials, or they're more concerned with other aspects of their ministry. Whatever their reason may be, training is a critical function in empowering volunteers to effectively administer their assigned responsibilities. However, before a solid training program can be established, you want to have two 'rights' in your ministry: the right people and the right program.

RIGHT PEOPLE

When selecting the right people, there are two things you must understand. First, members must be made into disciples of Jesus Christ before serving in any ministry. As a church leader and fellow disciple, this should be your first priority above all else.

And Jesus came and spake unto them, saying, All power is given unto me in heaven and in earth. Go ye therefore, and teach all nations, baptizing them in the name of the Father, and of the Son, and of the Holy Ghost: Teaching them to observe all things whatsoever I have commanded you: and, lo, I am with you always, even unto the end of the world. Amen.

MATTHEW 20:25-28

The body of Christ would probably agree that the commission Jesus gave His 11 disciples has been transferred to the church throughout the ages. Though many churches consider Matthew 28:18-20 to be the Great Commission, its fulfillment has been an omission in the lives of many believers.

Jesus' Great Commission should not be an omission in your life or ministry. Making disciples is a command, not a suggestion. And discipleship is not completed in a three to six-week New Believer's class.

With little experience as disciples of Christ, volunteers may not have enough spiritual insight, scriptural knowledge, or spiritual maturity to address the multitude of issues they may face. When problems do arise, they may reach back to their old ways in the flesh to address them. And as you may know, nothing good happens when people act in the flesh. (I'll mention how to know when a volunteer is properly trained in discipleship a bit later. A hint can be found in Matthew 7:15-20 and Luke 3:1-14, emphasis on verse eight).

YOU WANT DISCIPLES OF JESUS SERVING IN YOUR MINISTRIES.

The second thing you must understand for selecting the right people is that not every member in the church is ready, qualified, or called to serve in a ministry. You want volunteers that are ideally purposed for your ministry. Filling a vacancy with any available person just to keep the ministry going shouldn't be a priority.

When a church member is placed in a position not suited for them, a number of problems can occur, no matter how much training you provide them:

1. The volunteer may not be enthusiastic about serving in the ministry and may not give their best effort or focus to serving effectively (cf. John 10:12-13).

2. Those being served by the ministry may not receive the spiritual nourishment they truly need.

3. The volunteer may become agitated, angry, or frustrated with their leadership or those they serve because they're assigned to a ministry they don't want to be in.

4. The volunteer may decide to sabotage the ministry's efforts in order to be removed from their position, at the detriment of the members' well-being.

5. Because of the volunteer's frustrations, the members in the ministry may be

spiritually, emotionally, or even physically abused by the volunteer.

I don't think you want these issues in your ministry, but this is the chance you take each time you allow untrained or mismatched volunteers in your ministry. Maybe you'll need to allow a ministry position to go vacant or suspend ministry operations until the 'right' volunteer is identified. Believe me, it's much easier to have the right people, in the right positions, with the right training, at the right time. Be patient. God knows the needs of your ministry and will supply them at the right time.

RIGHT PROGRAMS

Training is a vital element to any assignment in ministry. It'll take a lot more than handing your volunteers a curriculum book to empower them toward a successful ministry experience. They should be equipped with the necessary information, tools, and resources to help them serve effectively.

Ministry training should be designed as a year-round program that properly equips your volunteers from the moment they enter the ministry until they depart. You want to outline a yearly training schedule and identify specific learning objectives based on the needs of your volunteers and the ministry as a whole.

Sometimes however, the level of training your volunteers require may be beyond your direct knowledge or expertise. Therefore, you'll need to research other training programs, ministries, and other seminars and conferences for training resources. There may also be a neighboring church ministry that could help you locate or provide training information and materials. They may even be willing to teach a series of lessons in your areas of need. Lastly, you should also consider sending a few volunteers to a local or national seminar or conference. These events can often provide a wealth of information, tools, and resources to further enhance the level of ministry provided to your volunteers.

BENEFITS OF TRAINING YOUR VOLUNTEERS

When you have the right people and program in your ministry, there are a number of benefits:

1. Equips volunteers with the information, tools, and resources to serve effectively.

2. Grows volunteers responsibly.

3. Builds confidence and competence among volunteers.

4. Standardizes learning principles and objectives across the ministry.

5. Establishes a structured and orderly flow of operations and support functions.

6. Provides an inviting ministry that other members would like to be a part of.

appreciation

Appreciation is a necessity in ministry. Your volunteers aren't being paid for serving. They're giving up their own free time, often away from their families. Your appreciation shows that you recognize your volunteers' achievements and sacrifices, while providing avenues of encouragement and support.

I want you to consider a time when you volunteered in ministry and you completed an important task, project, or run a successful ministry event and you received hardly any appreciation for your efforts. How did that make you feel? Did you feel full of appreciation and love? Probably not. Your confidence may have tanked. You could have become angry. Maybe you felt unappreciated or even wanted to quit. A lack of appreciation could have been draining every ounce of your motivation to continue serving in ministry.

REMEMBER...LOVE OTHERS AS YOURSELF.

WHAT CAN YOU DO TO APPRECIATE YOUR VOLUNTEERS?

1. Affirmation. Affirmation is considered as approval or acceptance from another person. From children to adults, people desire varying levels of affirmation. They want those around them in the workplace, home, church, etc. to accept them openly. Therefore, you should let your volunteers know how much their service is appreciated. A simple (and sincere) word of thanks and appreciation of their efforts can go a long way in motivating your volunteers, but that's just a start...

2. Gifts. There are a number of gifts you can provide to show your appreciation. A gift doesn't have to be extravagant or expensive to make a big impact, such as writing handwritten cards for birthdays and significant events in your volunteers' lives. A

handwritten note may seem like a simple gesture, but it says you're willing to take the time to appreciate them in a special way. Another gift idea is as inexpensive as making candy gift bags or giving away movie coupons and restaurant gifts certificates. You can even raffle off a vacation getaway.

3. Public Recognition. You can recognize your volunteers' service by highlighting certain milestones or creating a church recognition week or month, where church members share notes of love, praise, and appreciation on a large poster board or a wall dedicated to your volunteers. You may even host a volunteer recognition dinner in honor of those who have given their time and efforts to making your ministry a success.

4. Love. When your life and ministry is founded in love, you'll give freely and from a pure heart. Think for a moment about the people you love. How do you show your love toward them? How often? You may make a point to learn their favorite candy and food, favorite flowers, or even places they like to go. And whenever you're able, you'll shower

them with these items to show how much you love them.

When your appreciation for your volunteers is founded in love, you can give your time, money, and talents to prepare a home cooked meal, babysit their children so they can enjoy a little 'me' time, or even lead their ministry so they can attend a church service. These are small, yet powerful gestures to show how much you appreciate your volunteers. The only limitation is your own imagination and creativity.

Regardless of what you may do, it's important to communicate your appreciation of your volunteers' efforts in word and deed. They need to know how much they're appreciated as a valuable member of your ministry, and no one can do that better than you.

restoration

VOLUNTEERS ARE PEOPLE TOO.

There comes a season in every volunteer's life when a little time away from the ministry is needed. Volunteers are not robotic machines that can run endlessly from week to week without rest or relief. Without time to restore, volunteers can fall prey to exhaustion, frustration, and all manner of temptation and sin.

When these conditions arise, even the most committed volunteer will need time away from the ministry to reflect, repent (if necessary), and be restored. If you leave burned out, struggling, and frustrated volunteers serving in your ministry, numerous problems may arise, not only for the ministry, but possibly those being served and the church as a whole.

HURTING PEOPLE OFTEN HURT OTHERS.

You would save yourself many problems, heartache, and accountability to the Lord (for allowing those individuals to continue when in your care) by addressing the problem(s) immediately and allowing your volunteers the opportunity to be restored unto God.

When the children of Israel journeyed from mount Hor, they became discouraged (Numbers 21:4-5). They spoke against God and Moses concerning their journey out of Egypt and their lack of bread and water. The people said they loathed the light bread being given unto them. They allowed discouragement to begin a declining process of contempt against God. Consider how discouragement affected the Israelites:

1. Discouragement produced complaining.

2. Their complaining caused them to ignore God's blessings.

3. They rejected God's will for their lives.

4. They failed to bring glory to God.

5. Complaining spread a rebellious attitude and spirit in their hearts and minds.

6. Many people died as a result of their actions (Numbers 21:6).

ADDRESS ISSUES IMMEDIATELY BEFORE THEY SPREAD.

Volunteers may also need to be restored from demotivation. Even the most energetic volunteer and those specifically called to serve in a specific ministry can be affected by demotivation. They may reach a point where they stagnate or feel their service in the ministry is more like a prison sentence.

Though some volunteers may want to fight through their feelings and know they shouldn't be weary in well doing (cf. Galatians 6:9), their physical, emotional, and mental state continues to wane. When these moments arise, it's important they're allowed the opportunity and 'room' to refresh themselves. Sometimes, this period of refreshing may be a week or more, but they need time to recharge and refocus their life and purpose in the Lord without having to think about volunteering.

Come unto me, all ye that labour and are heavy laden, and I will give you rest. Take my yoke upon you, and learn of me; for I am meek and lowly in heart: and ye shall find rest unto your souls. For my yoke is easy, and my burden is light.

MATTHEW 11:28-30

In the process of restoration, you should remain visible, vocal, and compassionate. Provide the volunteer with the necessary counseling, training, support, affirmation, etc., in an environment separated from the ministry.

No matter how good your intentions are to bring restoration to your volunteers' lives, not everyone will appreciate spending time to work on themselves. Some volunteers may see your efforts as an attack on their growth in their personal ministry and in the Lord. However, they may not understand the impact of not addressing these issues early in their life and ministry. As their gift makes room for them and are brought before great men (cf. Proverbs 18:16), those great men will see their fall as their sin is exposed. Sadly, you may have seen this happen to many church leaders across the body of Christ because they didn't address their issues early on.

Before a prayerful decision is made on whether the volunteer will return to the ministry, their life should yield fruits worthy of repentance (in word and deed) (cf. Matthew 7:15-20; Luke 3:1-14, emphasis on verse eight). The fruit produced through their life should reveal their commitment to the Lord and whether it's in the best interests of the volunteer and/or the church to continue in the ministry, extend their restoration period, or be permanently removed.

Whether a decision is made to remove a volunteer or not, it's important for you to remain an active supporter in their life. Many church leaders have a habit of only caring for the 'ninety-nine' sheep in their congregation and leaving the one sheep to fend for themselves (cf. Matthew 18:12-14). These leaders do not call, text, visit, or check up on the volunteer at all. The volunteer is almost treated as an outcast because they're no longer 'useful' to the ministry.

Even if a volunteer never returns to your ministry or church, allow compassion to rule in your heart for them. Having a member leave your ministry doesn't excuse you or any other church leader from forgetting about them. Loving people shouldn't only be reserved for those in your church. You may not contact the volunteer everyday, but you should pray for them regularly and call, text, or visit them to ensure they are well. Remember, God loves the world, not just the members in your church, and so should you.

Allow the Lord to use you as a conduit to usher true freedom from sin, depression, heartache, and pains from their past. Some members' process of restoration will take years for them to be freed from their situations. They will need church leaders who are willing to patiently walk with them through their dark valleys; church leaders that will not give up on them; and church leaders that will serve them, pray unceasingly, can always be counted on, and refuse to become judgmental. Sometimes, people only need to know someone is cheering for their success.

Be kindly affectioned one to another with brotherly love; in honour preferring one another; Not slothful in business; fervent in spirit; serving the Lord; Rejoicing in hope; patient in tribulation; continuing instant in prayer; Distributing to the necessity of saints; given to hospitality.

ROMANS 12:10-13

conclusion

STAR Power is a brief discussion of four simple ways you can effectively minister to your church volunteers. Volunteers are an important part of any church ministry, and it's my sincerest prayer that this book has provided you with some important discussion points, tools, and principles to transform the level of support, training, appreciation, and restoration you provide them. Each ministry and church will have varying dynamics and methods for interacting with their volunteers, but the important thing is to engage with them and be proactive.

As your ministry extends to each member in your church, volunteers are not to be excluded. There may be volunteers around you right now that are silently suffering. They may feel alone, helpless, tired, and frustrated. Be fervent in supporting, training, appreciating, and restoring those who serve so that your church will be filled with beautiful and healthy volunteers to the glory of God. God bless.

notes

1 - Blue Letter Bible. "Dictionary and Word Search for plēsion (Strong's 4139)". Blue Letter Bible. 1996-2013. 1 May 2013. http://www.blueletter.org/lang/lexicon.cfm?Strongs=G4139&t=KJV

2 - Blue Letter Bible. "Dictionary and Word Search for diakonos (Strong's 1249)". Blue Letter Bible. 1996-2013. 5 May 2013. http://www.blueletter.org/lang/lexicon.cfm?Strongs=G4139&t=KJV

(com)mission
P U B L I S H I N G

www.commissionpubs.com
info@commissionpubs.com

www.ingramcontent.com/pod-product-compliance
Lightning Source LLC
Chambersburg PA
CBHW071752020426
42331CB00008B/2293